Uprooting Every Territorial Sorcerers

DS VOLUME 19

Bishop Climate Irungu

Copyright © 2016 by Bishop Climate Ministries

All rights reserved. No part of this publication may be reproduced, distributed or transmitted in any form or by any means, including photocopying, recording, or other electronic or mechanical methods, without the prior written permission of the publisher, except in the case of brief quotations embodied in critical reviews and certain other noncommercial uses permitted by copyright law. For permission requests, write to the publisher, addressed "Attention: Permissions Coordinator," at the address below.

Bishop Climate Ministries
PO Box 67884
London, England SE5 9JJ
www.bishopclimate.org
Email: prayer@bishopclimate.org
Tel: +44 7984 115900 (UK)
Tel: +44 207 738 3668 (UK)
Tel: +732 444 8943 (USA)

Contents

What is a Territorial Sorcerer? 3

4 Signs to Identify a Territorial Sorcerer in Your Life 10

5 Types of Territorial Sorcerers... 14

21 Prayer Points On

Uprooting Territorial Sorcerers... 17

What Can I Expect?.. 22

INTRODUCTION

Are you fed up of seeing others prosper despite their wicked ways? Are you tired of seeing others get ahead in life while you have been stuck in your situation for years? Are you tired of never getting rewarded for your good works? Well today something is about to change.

God revealed to me that somebody has been holding you hostage for a long time and now it's time for them to go. There is something that God wants to break, this extension of problems, delays, financial troubles, always waiting on money to come through but it keeps getting pushed forward. There is somebody that is always holding you up, dangling false hope, false dreams before you, so that you keep chasing after them, but it never resorts to anything. No that must be broken. Every prolonging of problems, sickness, disease, diagnosis, it must die by fire! Today we are dealing with the root of that problem.

CHAPTER ONE

What is a Territorial Sorcerer?

Now for some time a man named Simon had practiced sorcery in the city and amazed all the people of Samaria. He boasted that he was someone great, and all the people, both high and low, gave him their attention and exclaimed, "This man is rightly called the Great Power of God." They followed him because he had amazed them for a long time with his sorcery. (Acts 8:9-12)

A territorial sorcerer is a witch who has a spiritual control over a specific area; it could be your working place, your family, your neighbourhood, your city, etc.

Sorcery is a demonic power, it gives you something little but in return it takes so much. As long as this man was controlling that city, people were in bondage, no miracles were taking place; everyone was stuck spiritually.

When you have a sorcerer in your life it prevents you from moving forward; it will stop the plans of God for your life.

For a long time, I see that somebody has been bewitching you with sorcery. It's though you have been sleeping, your life has been clouded with darkness for so long that you can't even think. Inside your heart you are always thinking of where you could be, dreaming of greatness, but no matter what you try everything turns to nothing. I see there was some witchcraft, a sorcery that was released over your life when you were a small child. They saw that you were destined for greatness, that you were going to go high, and they wanted to stop you. But today we are going to break that spell.

Sometimes territorial sorcerers can be assigned into your life just to bring you down. I see that you were doing fine until that person came into your life, since then they have been bringing you down. Somehow, someway, they have been making you feel so small, like a nobody, like you are not worthy of them, and you end up hating yourself.

This happened to one woman who came to our ministry. For years she had been crippled and confined to her bed, her boyfriend had to do everything for her, cook her food, pick her up to go to the toilet, etc. until she came to our ministry and God set her free. But she realized that all of the issues she had faced began after this man came into her life. As long as he was around, nothing was progressing in her life. Yes he was there looking after her, but actually he was just controlling her, making sure that she never got on with her life.

But when she got rid of that man, all the pain left and now she's a free woman.

Whosoever loves to see you bound and helpless I command them to be exposed within the next 48 hours.

In the next chapter we read about one of the most important stories in the book of Acts. Saul, the man who had been persecuting anyone who preached about Jesus, was converted. And after that miracles began.

Then the church throughout Judea, Galilee and Samaria enjoyed a time of peace and was strengthened. Living in the fear of the Lord and encouraged by the Holy Spirit, it increased in numbers. As Peter traveled about the country, he went to visit the Lord's people who lived in Lydda. There he found a man named Aeneas, who was paralyzed and had been bedridden for eight years. "Aeneas," Peter said to him, "Jesus Christ heals you. Get up and roll up your mat." Immediately Aeneas got up. All those who lived in Lydda and Sharon saw him and turned to the Lord. (Acts 9:31-35)

This man was paralyzed for 8 years but he picked up his mat and walked.

I see that you should have gotten your breakthrough a long time ago, but there is a sorcerer that has been controlling and manipulating the resources and the people around you, they have been stopping them from getting to you, they have caused them to turn against you. But something is about to happen. Yes that mouth that has been biting you is about to come and bless you. Anyone that has been messing with you for a long time, today they must die by fire.

Sorcerers and witches are very wicked people. They can leave everything behind to give all their attention to you, focusing on making sure you don't move forward. It happened to Paul in the book of Acts:

Once when we were going to the place of prayer, we were met by a female slave who had a spirit by which she predicted the future. She earned a great deal of money for her owners by fortune-telling. She followed Paul and the rest of us, shouting, "These men are servants of the Most High God, who are telling you the way to be saved." She kept this up for many days. Finally Paul became so annoyed that he turned around and said to the spirit, "In the name of Jesus Christ I command you to come out of her!" At that moment the spirit left her. (Acts 16:16-18)

Here was a girl using the spirit of sorcery to earn money for her owners. But she left that to follow after Paul and the disciples. At first they might have thought she was only helping their cause, but Paul noticed as long as she was around, something was not right. Things were not moving forward. That spirit of sorcery was controlling the area where Paul was praying.

Territorial sorcerers are soothsayers; they talk sweet words to you to make you think that they have your best interest at heart, but deep down they are wicked; they have other intentions.

Something has been controlling you, manipulating you, closing your eyes to the truth. Your destiny is great but the spirit of sorcery has been dripping around your life for too long. There is a sorcerer who has been bewitching your family for a long time and it has caused such a shame, but whatsoever has been battling you for a long time, every form of sorcery that you have inherited from your mothers house, from your fathers house, today we are going to deal with them.

The Bible says that there was a great joy in the city once they were delivered from sorcery (Acts 8:8).

After today you are about to experience joy. God is a mighty God; yes there is a sorcerer today that God is going to strike with lightning, because enough is enough.

CHAPTER TWO

4 Signs to Identify a Territorial Sorcerer in Your Life

1) CONTROL & MANIPULATION

They insist on being in control. They like the feeling of being in power. They want to make sure you feel powerless without them. The man in Samaria was controlling the whole city. Before anyone made a decision they would have to come and consult him.

2) DELAY

Territorial sorcerers have no manners; they can sit in their office and control your money. Your documents could have come long time ago, your application could have been approved long time ago, but there is a sorcerer who is using witchcraft to control those documents, those finances. Sometimes you may need a document for a specific job, for school, for a contract, and its not coming because there is a sorcerer sitting there making sure it doesn't go through.

3) FALSE HOPE

Territorial sorcerers love to give false hope. They give you false promises so that you believe in them but you end up disappointed and worse off than before. You may think that this person is from God so you keep allowing them in your life, but this person is not from God, they are a demonic agent sent from hell to keep you in bondage.

4) PRIDE

They are always boasting about how big they are, how powerful they are, how successful they are. They want you to know that you can't live without them, that you need them in order to get what you are after; they like feeling like a king or queen and making you feel small.

I see there is an institutional sorcerer, someone sitting somewhere to block everything that has to do with you. These are people assigned by the devil to bring delay, in order to cause disappointment and denial. But right now as I speak to you, any sorcerer that is in the system, who has been hired in order to block you and cause sabotage in your life, as long as the Lord lives, they are going to die by fire!

A few weeks ago I was supposed to have some money come through so I called the bank but it had not shown up in the account yet. The Lord showed me that there was a sorcerer sitting on my money so I prayed and called back an hour later. It was there.

From now on I declare that every document is coming flying to you, whatever you need, any title deed, any application that you need, any money that you need, it is coming your way, no more delay in Jesus name.

CHAPTER THREE

5 Types of Territorial Sorcerers

1) INSTITUTIONAL

There are territorial sorcerers working in the government controlling the resources, controlling the finances, controlling the laws, etc. They can cause delay and rejection in applications. Many organized institutions like schools and universities are headed by demonic powers. They can prevent you from getting into a specific school or program, causing delay and failure in your life or children's lives.

2) CITY/NEIGHBOURHOOD

When there is a territorial sorcerer or witch in your neighborhood it can affect your family. You find someone is always harassing your children, teachers picking on them in school, and no matter what you try to do it seems every door is shut. You can experience a lot of injustice.

3) FAMILY

Some territorial sorcerers can be assigned to families for generations. Making sure nobody ever succeeds in life, nobody ever makes it past graduation, and nobody ever has a happy family. The whole family is plagued. School dropouts, career dropouts, marriage dropouts, and every other form of drop outs associated with failure.

4) CORPORATE WORLD

There are territorial sorcerers that control companies; they control regions. They control the economy;

they block and blacklist those who have been called to shine. When there is a sorcerer in your working place, strange things happen. You feel targeted, you feel so afraid as though you don't belong there. Sometimes you can't even go to work, you have trouble sleeping.

5) FINANCIAL

Territorial sorcerers can cause poverty. They come and bewitch a place so that nothing can develop. Sometimes when I am travelling I can tell which places are controlled by sorcery because I see entire areas where nothing is finished. Projects are started but they stop half way.

21 PRAYER POINTS ON

Uprooting Territorial Sorcerers

efore you pray, remember to put on the full armor of God according to Ephesians 6:10-18, touching each part of your body as you say it.

Repeat with me: "I put on the full armor of God. The helmet of salvation upon my head, the breastplate of righteousness in its place, the belt of truth around my waist, my feet shod with the readiness of the gospel of peace, taking the shield of faith in my left hand and the sword of the spirit in my right."

In the Name of Jesus:

1. Every territorial sorcerer in my family that has been causing none of us to move forward, I bind you, I rebuke you, die by fire!

2. Every territorial sorcerer over my life, over my land, my houses, my investments, my career, my family, my business, I bind you, I bind you, I bind you, I rebuke you, die by fire, die by fire!

3. Every sorcerer that has been causing trouble in my life, over my children, my health, my career, I bind you, I rebuke you, I command you to die by fire!

4. Every sorcerer in my father's house, in my mother's house, in my wife/husband's house, I bind you, I rebuke you, and I command you to die by fire!

5. Every sorcerer that has been disturbing my

sleep, my health, my children, marriage, business or career, I bind them in Jesus name!

6. Every sorcerer in my working place that has been making work so difficult for me, I rebuke you, I bind you, I command you to die by fire!

7. Every territorial sorcerer that has been sitting on my promotion and tarnishing my good name, I rebuke you in Jesus name!

8. Every institutional sorcerer that has been sitting on my documents, causing delay in my applications, die by fire!

9. Every sorcerer who is staying in my house, taking control of my car, controlling my children, controlling my finances, I command them to die by fire!

10. Every sorcerer in my neighborhood that has been bringing bad luck, I rebuke you, I bind you, die by fire!

11. Every sorcerer who has been following my children, harassing them, bewitching them day by day, die by fire!

12. Every sorcerer that has been bewitching my marriage and/or relationships, I command them to die by fire!

13. Every curse of good beginnings and bad ending it must end today. So every sorcerer that has caused me to never finish what I start, I break its powers in Jesus name. From today, I will finish what I start.

14. Every sorcerer over my finances, over my career, my business, my contracts, I bind you, I rebuke you, die by fire!

15. Every sorcerer that has been controlling my life, that has shut my finances, that has shut my life, I break your powers in the name of Jesus.

16. As from today I declare and I decree I am an overcomer. I break free from every territorial witch attached to my destiny.

17. Today I declare and decree that everyday in every way I am becoming a money magnet.

18. Today I declare and decree that everyday in every way I am becoming a success magnet.

19. Today I declare and decree that everyday in every way I am becoming a wealth magnet.

20. Today I declare and decree that everyday in every way I am becoming a good health magnet.

21. Today I declare and decree that everyday in every way I am becoming a good life magnet.

CONCLUSION

What Can I Expect?

So now that you have your prayer points you need to understand that deliverance is not a onetime event but a process and you need to be consistent if you are going to destroy the enemies in your life. Let's look at a few things you can expect while going through your deliverance.

Firstly, expect to be set free and for peace to return back into your life. The Bible says that those who wait for the Lord shall not be ashamed. Also, start expecting God to give you a testimony, just like everyone else who has gone through our deliverance program.

There are some key steps you can follow to ensure you are doing everything properly in order to obtain your desired goals. (These are in addition to your daily prayer points listed in this book)

1. <u>Locate the area of your need</u>

According to what your situation may be, you need to identify the particular area or areas, which are most dire.

2. <u>Find out what the Word of God says regarding that area</u>

Select the appropriate scriptures promising you what you desire and meditate upon them. Write them on your walls where you can see them. Even if it means writing it on yourself so you won't forget to recite them during the day. Do whatever it takes but make sure you are replaying them in your mind daily.

3. <u>Go through a special prayer in one of the following ways while expecting your deliverance</u>

· 3 day Night Vigil at the Sanctuary (i.e. praying and confessing the Word from 10 pm to 5 am for 3 nights in a row)

· 3 Day Fast (i.e. praying, fasting, and confessing the Word daily from 6 am to 6 pm for 3 days. Alternatively you can fast straight through the 3 days only breaking for communion)

· 3-Day Fast Prayer Vigil at the Sanctuary (i.e. praying, fasting, and confessing the Word daily from 10 am to 6 pm for 3 days. Again you can fast continually for 3 days apart from communion)

· 3 + Days Dry Fast (i.e. praying, fasting, and confessing the Word for 3 or more days without taking food or drink). Please note: This should only be done under pastoral recommendation.

4. Pray aggressively while believing that you receive your deliverance

Hebrews 11:6 says *"we must believe that He is and that He is a rewarder of them that diligently seek Him".*

5. Make any adjustments in your life and repent as the Holy Spirit leads

You have to make sure that you are not leaving any open doors for the enemy to regain access in your life.

6. This is the most crucial step. You must sow your seed to seal your deliverance

Most people sow consecutive seeds, giving it the same name according to their expectation from God regarding their deliverance. To truly succeed in spiritual warfare you have to be a sower. The Bible says in Deut 16:16 to "never appear before God empty handed". So as you are expecting to receive something from

God you need to be giving back something to Him as well.

7. Lastly, prepare yourself for your miracle physically and spiritually

Be vigorous in attending service as much as possible in order to receive the ministration of the Word and the laying on of the hands by the man of God. Also, attend your deliverance sessions regularly if you have been assigned to a mentor.

ABOUT THE MINISTRY

Bishop Climate Ministries is the Healing & Deliverance Ministry founded by Bishop Climate under the anointing and direction of the Holy Spirit. God has anointed Bishop Climate with incredible power to set the captives free. Many people who were unable to get deliverance anywhere else find their freedom as they attend special deliverance sessions conducted through this ministry. The vision of Bishop Climate Ministries is to reach over 1 billion people with the message of deliverance and prosperity, especially in understanding the things of the spirit. Many people are bound because of lack of knowledge and one of the goals of this ministry is to set people free through education.

A PERSONAL NOTE FROM THE AUTHOR

Child of God I want you to know how much I appreciate you and how special you are to me. That is why God keeps giving me the wisdom to write these books at such a time as this. He sees your heart and wants you to experience the abundant life that Jesus died for. And so do I. Your support for our ministry is crucial and I hope that you will always continue to lift us up in prayer to God.

I want to take this opportunity to encourage you to partner with us at Bishop Climate Ministries. Hundreds have testified of the miracles that have taken place in their life just as a result of sowing into this ministry and I want you to be able to experience that 100 fold return Jesus spoke about regarding sowing seed into good ground. The Bible says in Proverbs 11:24 *"One person gives freely, yet gains even more; another withholds unduly, but comes to poverty"*. Your prayers and financial support are crucial to take this message of salvation and deliverance around the world. And as you do that you can be sure that God is going to bless you beyond your wildest imaginations. There is a 4-fold anointing that you step under when you become a partner with Bishop Climate Ministries. It is the anointing that God has put over my life and this ministry according to Isaiah 11:2. That is the anointing of Divine Direction, Divine Connections, Divine Provision and Divine Protection.

Please understand how much I value you. Your support for our ministry is so crucial and your prayers are as a pillar to us. Your partnership with this ministry is so important and that's why we are committed to praying for you daily and lifting your needs up before God. When you send in your donation please send me a prayer request as well so I can intercede on your behalf before God. I look forward to seeing you in person at our Healing and Deliverance Centre in London, England or at one of our Healing and Deliverance Miracle Crusades.

Remember this is the Ministry where the captives are set free and souls are refreshed.

Remain blessed,

Bishop Climate Irungu

MORE TITLES FROM OUR DELIVERANCE SERIES

Victory Over The Spirit Of Humiliation & Oppression
Breaking The Curse Of
Good Beginnings & Bad Endings
Victory Over Demonic Assignments
Overcoming Every Generational Hatred
Overcoming Persistent Enemies
Destroying Every Demonic Blockage
Victory Over Every Troubling Spirit
Destroying Every Spirit of Poverty & Lack
Destroying Every Demonic Covenant Over Your Life
Victory Over Every Appointment With Death
Binding the Strongman
Uprooting Every Demonic Prophecy
Victory Over Every Evil Wish
Breaking Every Demonic Spell
Overturning Every Demonic Judgment
Victory Over Every Frustrating Spirit
Destroying Every Demonic Altar
Uprooting Every Territorial Sorcerers

Victory Over Demonic Storms (Marine Spirit)
Dealing With the Spirit of Disappointment
Victory Over The Lying Spirit

Order Enquiries: Please call our offices or order online at www.bishopclimate.me

Bishop Climate Ministries

P.O. Box 67884, London, SE5 9JJ
England, United Kingdom
Tel: +44 7984 115900
Email: partners@bishopclimate.org

Yes Bishop! I am breaking free once and for all and I am sowing my seed of Divine Liberation of £70.

I have enclosed my special seed of deliverance
£ _____

Here is my Prayer request covering the 7 areas I desire the Lord to manifest His Miracles in my life:

_____

_____

_____

_____

_____

_____

_____

(Continued on Back)

Name:

_____

Address:

_____

_____

_____

Telephone:

_____

Email:

_____

NOTE: You can also sow your special seed SAFELY &
SECURELY online via
www.bishopclimate.org/donate.aspx

Printed in Great Britain
by Amazon